E...Motions

by
Carol Livernois-Mitchell

authorHOUSE™

1663 LIBERTY DRIVE, SUITE 200
BLOOMINGTON, INDIANA 47403
(800) 839-8640
WWW.AUTHORHOUSE.COM

First published by AuthorHouse 02/17/05

ISBN: 978-1-4208-3068-2 (sc)
ISBN: 978-1-4634-8563-4 (e)

Library of Congress Control Number: 2005901303

Printed in the United States of America
Bloomington, Indiana

This book is printed on acid-free paper.

All Poetry has been written by: Carol Livernois-Mitchell

Table of Contents

All The Time

I am missing you
I find my current thoughts of other men being replaced by thoughts of you.
I'm missing you.
What have I done?
Am I opening a can of worms?
My life is changing. The morals I once used to have, are fading.
I'm missing you, so.
I miss your sweet kisses.
I miss your thoughtfulness.
I miss your Southern Charm.
Yes, I'm missing you.
I want to share my morning coffee with you, all the time.
I want to sit on that bench at the ocean with you, all the time.
I want to extend words of encouragement to you, always
Ah yes, I am missing you.

As My Mind Wanders

As I lie in my bed, my secluded thoughts are with you.
Even though you are 65 miles away, my thoughts are with you.
As you are sound asleep.
I envision myself so close to your body that nothing could fit between us
My arm wrapped around your body, holding you so close
That my breasts are embedded into your back
As I give you butterfly kisses upon your shoulder
I hear a soft groan, as if an insect had disturbed your sleep
I see your lip quiver for only a second
Am I invading a private thought of yours?
Am I invading a dream that is happening?
Perhaps, a dream that you may not remember
Could it ever be about me?
It doesn't matter
For I'm sure I am dreaming
You pay no mind to me. I am just a buddy.
But I can dream, can't I?
I will keep my dream to myself
I do not have to share it with anyone.
Notice, I am sharing it with you
As it was you in that dream

Back to Massachusetts

Oh how my thoughts have drifted home, several times
Thoughts of you captivate my very being
Flirting, I am, with thoughts of you missing me. Do you?
Oh how my thoughts have drifted to wishing we had spoken
During the last few days
Thoughts of speaking to you, of hearing your voice overwhelm me.
I want to hear all the positive things you consistently tell me.
I do miss you.
I missed you that very day, before I even left!
Hoping we will be together soon, my soul craves your embrace.
Maybe, if I close my eyes, my thoughts will put me there, for now.
I have been untouched since we were together
I will keep it that way, till we're together again.

Being Shot At

In the battlefield of love I stood
Shots being fired at me constantly
I stood there and deflected them
Because I loved you
The fight was never ending
I couldn't die
My love was too strong

Then the lies were being shot at me
Consistently
You couldn't tell me the truth anymore
You believed I would be angry if you lied?
Why did I stand in the field so long
Getting pop shots constantly

I can't take it anymore
I must leave the battle field now and move
on

Carol Livernois-Mitchell

Balloon Ride

Step into my balloon with me
So we can fly away
There will only be just me and you
We'll be gone for just one day

We'll fly over sun and sea
Rainbows high above
The ride we'll take
Is not of fate, but really made from love

The color red is dark and deep
Reminding of the heart
I'm sorry you're so far away
And we're so far apart

That's why this ride will mean a lot
To only you and I
The colors are so beautiful
As lovely as the sky

The pact we make for only us
No one will ever know
For in your heart, you always care
You always let that show

But all good things must come to end
No different would this ride be
But this balloon will never pop
Cause it's just you and me

My love for you just runs too deep
I'm sure you somehow know
True colors, rainbows, high above
I'll always love you so!

Bye

You used me, abused me, made me feel so low
Then you cry and tell me
That you have no place to go
I have done all that I could
To help you get along
Every argument that's ensued
It's me that's in the wrong
I used to have these feelings
That to no one else compared
Now it's time for you to leave
Deny me, if you dare!

Carol Livernois-Mitchell

Affections

Why are you so selfish with your affections?
One would think that, unless you are socially dysfunctional, you would enjoy
having your hand held, or maybe given a kiss goodnight
I cannot for the life of me, understand why one would be so selfish
I need you to hold my hand and give me a kiss on my cheek
I need you to hold me and give me a big hug
I need to be told that I am more than a friend
Why would I try to find someone in my life, if not to share?
I don't mean material things I mean affections as well

I have two men that I know would give me the affections that I need
They are married
I wouldn't want my affections stolen from anyone, nor would I steal their
affections toward their wives. It is not fair.
Please reconsider. I don't want this precious time to have been spent in vain.
It has been six weeks now.
At the beginning, you did have kind words, now those words have dissipated.
The emotional side of you has diminished. What have I done?
Is it me?
Please let me know.

I can't live without those little gestures of affection. It is just like a flower
with no water or sun, crying, trying to stand tall, but unable to, because of
weakness. I am that flower right now.
I am needing the warmth of your sunlight, the strength of that downpour of rain.
I need your affections.

Could you share them, please?

Christmas Wish

What I want for Christmas
Is not beneath my tree
I want you to love me
Love me...and only me
I sit and watch the lights so bright
High upon my tree
Christmas is so very lonely
Cause you're not here with me
Two people need to share this time
As special people do
For what I want this Christmas
You know,
It's really you!

Confusion

Whirlwinds of confusion surround my inner being
For the life of me I continue to wonder
Missing you was what I didn't want to happen
Missing you is consuming every thought I have
Feeling like each day is longer than the last
My heart aches for you, like it should not do
The latest words spoken between us are shaky
I want to believe you but I can't
So many lies spoken in years past
Many more lies in the future, I'm sure
You forget how well I know you
You forget how much I miss you but try not to
I want to wipe this slate clean and I can not
Why is that? Why do thoughts of you continue to haunt me
Every day, every waking moment of my life
I'm at the point that my stomach feels sick, constantly
Help me to end this fatal attraction
A fatal attraction that is taking over my life
Like a whirling dervish, hear me cry for help!

Congratulations

Dedicated to my parent's very dear friends for their 50th wedding anniversary. We love you both, Doris and Angelo

Congratulations to you both
On this very special day
Fifty years is a long time
Together for to stay

This special time of course deserves
Hearty congratulations
After all for 50 years you've put up
With all of your relations

You have a daughter and a son
They love you very much
For fifty years you have put up
With teenagers antics and such

You're two very special people
Great friends and parents too
I'd like to tell you at this time
I think the world of you

Don't Stop the Rain

Is it still raining in Maine, I asked?
That was weeks ago
We've grown friendly during these weeks
I poured out my heart and soul to you
I told you of loneliness, dinner parties, movies I had seen and with whom
I've learned about a wife that calls you names and makes derogatory comments
We discussed children and pets, our favorite colors and foods
We've talked about jobs and working, who is important and who isn't
How often you work, what a great garden you have and how unappreciative
Some people can be
No work for either of us this weekend, which means we are free to be
You and me
Yes, we took advantage of these wonderful hours
How special you made me feel. How much I enjoyed your company
Will this ever happen again?
I hope it will
A special moment in time,
Because I needed to know if it was still raining

Dreaming

Come lay down beside me
Put your body close to mine
I'll get us some munchies
And grab a glass of wine

I feel your heartbeat, against my chest
It feels so right to me
No one else could take your place
It's where I want to be

Kiss me softly where you may
My heart's yours without a doubt
Craving you for so long
This is what our love's about

This will be a chance we'll take
To me it's worth a try
I want to be with you so bad
I almost need to cry

Carol Livernois-Mitchell

Empty Thoughts

Like the winds of March
My feelings blow by you
Unaware of my inner self
How strong I can be
You're oblivious to anything
Consumed by your own being
Selfishness contained within
A heart of steel to only some
Passion so desired by one
Needlessly kept away from me
How distasteful one becomes
After so long of loving
The bittersweet taste
Left within me
For only you

Even If

Excitement that I'm feeling
Is much too high today
I'll have some stolen moments
When you come my way

Stolen moments of your time
Is all you have to give
I don't really like that much
It's an awful way to live

Because you are so special
The caring person, I see
I'm glad that you have set aside
This special time for me

Eye Candy

From the nape of your neck
To the small of your back
The strongest of shoulders
Draped merely diagonally
By only a white sheet
What still perfection to watch
As you slept my eyes were focused
Unlabored breaths sweetly emitted
From your lips
Perfection of the most beautiful of scenery
Better than on a canvas of color
Comparable to nothing else at that moment

Far Away

Please put my hand into your hand
And take me far away
Take me to the place I love
The place where I can play

My emotional dimension
Is ready to erupt
Wanting you to be near
You're far away; it's tough

I want you to be with me
In hours of the dawn
I need for you to hold me
My feelings can't be wrong

Embers burn deep in my heart
For it's you that can ignite them
With time that's past, I know you can
Those feelings never left...for I remember when

Fifteen Days

for my significant other John

Fifteen days but who's counting
I find myself missing you more and more
Obviously my feelings were not reciprocated
That of course means you've lied to me
I miss my hand in yours
I miss being wrapped up in your arms
I miss watching you sleep
I miss all of you
I am assuming this relationship is over
How saddened I am
I was beginning to love you more
More than I did three years ago
I will leave you alone
Hopefully, I can make peace within myself
I still love you more than ever
I think I always will
You have a piece of my heart

Flickering Flame

Out of nowhere there he was
From high school days of old
I often wondered where he was
"Very married" I was told

When we were young and wild and free
So much fun we had
I knew his Mom disliked me
Cause she was always mad!

We both worked in the hospital
Sneaking kisses when no one looked
We got along; oh yes we did
And both of us were hooked!

Searching our emotions high
To find out who we were
We loved each other very much
And this we knew for sure

All those days seem long ago
Forever in my heart
When we departed separate ways
We each made brand new starts

He showed up on the Internet
Much to my surprise
I'll always remember his great smile
And warm and loving eyes

Carol Livernois-Mitchell

Heartbroken

You broke my heart today

I thought we'd be together

My heart was jumping for joy

No call, you left without me

You weren't there

I was going to share the sunshine today

Instead, I had clouds over my head

She got the sun

She had your thoughts

I had nobody to share my day

I was heartbroken

You knew that

As you know me so well

We are together so little as it is

I hate when we're apart

I miss you more and more each week

We need to fix this somehow, some way

My heart can only take so much at one time

Heartsick

You told me you'd be here
Your promise was in my heart
I got sick but knew I'd be up and running
By the time you got here
You were my will
But you told me you'd be here
You weren't
My heart was smashed into a million tiny pieces
I believed you
The promise was made 2 months ago
And, I believed you
My heart and soul wanted to believe you
You called
But you told me you'd be here
I wanted you here
I wanted your arms holding me
I wanted your sweet kisses on my face
I needed you to kiss my tears away
I'm lost without you
I've loved you for what seems like an eternity
You promised to be here
I felt empty and betrayed and heartsick
But you told me you'd be here
YOU WEREN'T

I Can't Wait

Four days have passed. Where are you?
I miss your voice. I need to hear you
My spirits lifted from your thoughtfulness
You care...always. Happy or sad, you're there
I feel your thoughts. I'm unable to answer
Can you hear me? Can you feel my thoughts?
Mail came today. From you, my Sweetheart
I knew your writing instantly
I felt your hand in mine. I feel you breathing in my soul
So very far away, but really very close
My heart aches for your company
Your presence, your heart, your laughter
I need to be part of your life
I know I am, even though far away
One more week, six days exactly
Six more days I will see you. I will connect to you
In some small way, we will be closer
My Lion will roar and I will hear him
I will learn, listen and keep the red balloon afloat
I will keep on loving you
I can't wait

I Want To Be

I want to be the sunshine in your life
I want to be the rain to wash your troubles away
I want to be the cloud that protects you from harm
I want to be the wind to blow away your problems
I want to be the snow that covers you as a blanket does
I want to be the moon that shines your dark nights
I want to be the stars that shine for you consistently
I want to be all this and everything to you
Please let me?

Carol Livernois-Mitchell

Saturday Night Thoughts

Another Saturday night alone.
My thoughts are with you again
Are you missing me as much as I am missing you?
I want to believe that you are
I look forward to next weekend
I will be held by you
Embraced by those strong arms
I will be put into the arms I love
I will surrender to you
Letting me know that you missed me, as well
The excitement of time with you surrounds me
I need to share with you
I have words of love for you
I have your needs covered
I need you to talk to me
I need you to want me
My feelings are growing stronger
My heart is in your hands for safe keeping
Please hold me and never let me go

I'm Yours

To the highest of mountains
And the lowest of tides
I always want you
Right here by my side

Through thick and through thin
From high and to low
I want you to always
Remain as my beau

I want you, I need you
I can't live without
You're one of the best
To me, there's no doubt

We'll walk together
With your hand in mine
No words will be spoken
To me, you're divine

Please tell me you'll keep me
I won't ever tell
You'll be my beau always
And I'll be your belle

Carol Livernois-Mitchell

Imaginary Lover

My imaginary lover is what you have become
I just can't get you out of my head
There is too much fog in the way
What used to be real is now gone
What we had was so wrong
But at the time, it felt so right
It is now just a memory of love
The roughness of your hand against my skin
Your heartbeat against mine
You brought me down with words
You had to leave
What can I do now- but imagine
You have become
In my head
My imaginary lover
That's where you will stay

It Can Not Ever Be

We cannot and will not have each other
I have known you for a while
I catch those fleeting stolen glances
I sometimes hear what you're saying without you saying anything aloud
I know you've been reading my eyes and hearing what my heart is saying, as well
It cannot ever be!
Too many 'others' involved
I know you can read my passions
I know that you know what I want and need
It can never be!
Always lifting my spirits, thank you.
Trying to tell me, I'm not who I think I am
Just always finding the good in me, thank you
Personally, I think you deserve to have someone passionate around you
But, it can never be
Would it last? I think not. It's just the need that's there
I know the fire could be put out very easily
But, it cannot ever be!

Carol Livernois-Mitchell

It's People Like You

It's people like you that make people like me want to drink all the time
It's people like you that make people like me want to drink more than Pepsi or wine

It's people like you that make people like me think how disgusting men can be
It's people like you that make people like me think how trust is the key

It's people like you that make people like me make it hard to want to let go
It's people like you that make people like me find that love is so hard to show

It's people like you that make people like me, feel like a loser inside
It's people like you that make people like me, want to crawl in a hole and just die!

It's people like you that make people like me, have to learn a strong lesson
It's people like you that make people like me, have Al-anon for an every night session!

It's people like you that make people like me, think that they can NOT trust
It's people like you that make people like me, know that drinking, for you, is a must

It's people like you that make people like me see how you 'rip-off' a girl
It's people like you that make people like me, want to glue you inside of a pearl!

It's people like you that make people like me, not understand stupid men
It's people like you that make people like me learn how to come to the end!

Jim P.

With pen in-hand, I sit here
And ponder over him
We have become good friends, you know
Yes, his name is Jim

I think about him often
Wondering what's up today
He's very busy working
Doesn't take much time to play

His effect on me is calming
Knowing just what to say
Spending anytime with him
Would really make my day

We talk on the phone for hours
Words are never a loss
He's a very caring person
Even worrying about his boss!

He's the father of two children
That he loves with all his heart
I hear loneliness in his voice
If they have to be apart

His words are of encouragement
I hear it in his voice
I'm glad that he's a friend of mine
I know I've made a good choice

I'd like to stay his friend for life
Hoping this is his wish too
Friends are special people
Just like me and you

Carol Livernois-Mitchell

Jo-Jo Frazer

This cat was as big as a raccoon! The veterinary clinic liked him and sent us a sympathy card, which I thought was a very nice gesture on their part and very much appreciated by our family.

I had this little kitty cat
And Jo-Jo was his name
He was all mean and tough, you know
He never would play games
He'd look for food most anytime
The canned ones were the best
Twenty pounds put in a bag
Was all his to detest
He had a big old happy life
Nobody can deny
How did he live for 18 years?
Everyone asks why
He had not teeth to speak of
His claws cut long ago
His fur was always matted
He weighted 40 pounds or so
He growled more than dogs I know
It really made us laugh
Men were not his favorite
His attitude was half
Jo-Jo will be missed by all
Of us here in our house
He only sat and ate and drank
And never caught a mouse!
We will miss him very much
To put him down was tough
Everyone feels very badly
Talking about this stuff
They sent a card to say they care
Much to our surprise
Jo-Jo was a special cat
At least in our eyes

Journal Entry of Saturday, July 24, 2000

Woke up the first time at 5:45 AM. It was a bit chilly, so I turned off the fan. Of course, I slept in my favorite spot, the couch! My first thought this morning was back home with my friend, Jim. I figured that he must have been getting ready for those soccer games today.

I lied back down on the couch and awoke again at 6:45. Still too early to get up, but still wondered if Jim was on his way, by now to Springfield, MA. I remember those days, long ago, of being a soccer Mom. I graduated from soccer to football, which I detest! Bet, being a "Mom", I followed through. Did you know I was the only Mom sitting on those bleachers that fall? It was so cold! I was 6 months pregnant, but I was the Mom and stuck it out. Ah, what we do for our children.

Back to my next thought...the game has begun, as it is now 8:45 AM. I hope they win both games today. It's so nice to see a father's involvement. I never had that while I was married. He only came because he felt that he *had* to. It was always a chore for my children's father to go to anything that involved the children. What a sad thing. My Dad was always there for me and I still miss him terribly.

As I sit here this morning and look around my yard, I think some work needs to be done. Grass needs to be mowed and I can't wait until this porch is all together. My thoughts are also directed to Colorado this morning. Thoughts of a letter sent that I still couldn't believe I read. For the very first time in my life, I received and 'erotic\ [prose-like letter. The words were a little too strong in parts, but individuality counts here. Funny how people change. This letter was a bit embarrassing, but to the point. This is a part of him that I did not see 35 years ago.

Now my thoughts have darted to Ohio. How devastated Mark must be feeling today. My heart is with him. I think some prayer may help. I, being so far away, feel helpless. I wish I could help in some small way. Hence, my reason for sending poetry to him, acknowledging how important he is as a person and how much he means to other people. He's still important to his sons. I still think there may be more to this story than I know. It's not my business, so therefore, I will butt-out! It's now 9:10 AM and I am waiting for Pepere' so that we can go to the ocean. I can drown my thoughts in those crashing waves. I can share my most intimate thoughts with that ocean' and the words will never be repeated, nor will my thoughts!

Journal Entry of September 23, 2000

It has been a very difficult, trying week. Other than writing two very short poems and a four page letter to my friend Mark, I have spent most of today, crying.

I wish I knew why I was so upset inside. For one thing, I could have been in Ohio this weekend, but that was then, this is now. I am here. I lost a baby 32 years ago, today. I am missing Bobby Lawrence, I hate my job, my kids don't need me and I don't know why I am here! I need to sell my trailer and don't want to.

I decided to go for a ride. I am now (at 3:52 PM) sitting at Pine Point, Maine. The seagulls are flying, boats are drifting, there is a man walking with his Cocker Spaniel, which is probably his best friend. Today, I am missing one of those. I'm very lonely and upset. Two people are kayaking. The water is still and it is very tranquil here. It's no wonder my mother wanted a ride to Hampton Beach, New Hampshire to see the ocean waters one more time before her death. That episode was four days before she passed away.

I think I will take a ride to the mall. I'd like to have something new for myself. However, I sort of whish I were that one seagull out there, which is just floating wherever the wind is pushing it.

Why can't my life be like that?

Journal Entry of Saturday, October 7, 2000
10:59 AM

Back at Pine Point, I find myself. Today as least I am not crying, nor am I feeling upset, at all.

There are about one dozen fishing boats anchored out here. It is still, calm and quiet except for the distant sound of a boat engine, echoing. On the other side of this part of the ocean, fall is making its debut. The colors are more intent than they were the last time I was here. I notice that the colors to the left of me are lighter and brighter shades of gold, magenta and yellow. The colors to my right are darker, deeper shades of red, orange and maroon.

It's not a very sunny day today. Clouds are hovering over these fishing boats with the sun trying to break through them. I see people fishing off the pier and I remember when I used to go fishing with my Dad. Fishing was one of his favorite things to do. I wonder if it was the peace and tranquility that brought him there. I must be my father's daughter!

At this time, the tide is out. Ripples are dancing softly upon an ocean that nature can make stronger and angrier than any of us could imagine. Alas, the sun has come through the clouds, making today a beautiful fall day.

Among the nature available to my sight, is a hibiscus bush. I wonder how those beautiful little white flowers have survived the uneven temperatures that only the change of seasons can deliver. They're so strong, not wilted, as one would expect.

From the boat dock, just emerged two men looking like "GI Joes" in full army apparel. The part that makes me chuckle is that even their fishing boat is painted in camouflage. One has to wonder if they were ever in the armed services or just "GI Joe" want-to-be's

Two young adults, I would guess to be about 14 yrs of age, are learning the art of a sling shot, as they stop to pull their kayak into the water.

This parking spot as you can tell, is one of my favorite places to be. There are so many sights, in such little time. To see the wonders that God has created, on this most beautiful fall day.

I did get out of my vehicle to ask those 2 men in their army clothes why they were dressed like that and had their boat to match. I was told that it was duck/ geese season and they would blend in with the scenery. Don't laugh, but even their ammunition bag was camouflaged!

Carol Livernois-Mitchell

Just a Pebble on the Beach

The emptiness I feel within
I never can explain that
To you, I am one pebble on the beach
The beach of loneliness
You are too busy for me
I am not the princess that you are looking for
I am just me, that lonely pebble of thousands
Not the 'special' one that you want
Just that one in a pile of millions
Don't worry about me
Before you were there, others walked on me
After you are gone, there will be more
More of the same
The ones that walk on you barefoot
After all, I am just one
Just one of those pebbles on the beach

Just Wondering

On Sunday morning
I will wait for you
My body will be flirting with thoughts
Thoughts of your embrace
I will be craving your affections,
As a person craves his drugs
I have missed you.
I have missed your sweet kisses
I have missed your soft caresses
the strength of your manhood
Holds a candle to none.
I miss our conversations of importance
Conversations of non-importance, as well.
I guess I just miss everything about you.
I will wait for you...
On Sunday morning

Carol Livernois-Mitchell

Love of My Life

This is in memory of my very best friend, Bobby Lawrence, who passed away on 11/11/99. He was only 50 yrs old and was the most talented person I have ever met in my life. I will forever miss his talent and true friendship. I will love him until the day that I die.

When I was 13, you were my dream come true
When I was 14, I knew I wanted to belong to you
When I was 15, we were together all the time
When I was 16, I told everyone that you were mine

At 17, you told me what I didn't care to hear
At 18, you were heavily into drugs, alcohol and beer
At 19, I went and had my first baby
I had another man, you had someone else, maybe

At 20 years old, we were still friends
We promised each other we'd e friends to the end
Through 30's and 40's we struggled along
Without each other we'd still here 'our' songs

Some of your habits, were not approved
Many times you just got up and moved
I got married too many times
But deep in my heart, you were always mine

I was with you last weekend and I had a ball
We sewed, had dinner, played piano and all
This week you left me without saying good-bye
We promised forever, now I'm asking, why?

Love Songs

Those soft nylon curtains blowing gently
The long old window from this old worn down hotel
Sun shining ever so brightly from the beautiful sky
I hear sounds of Andrea Bocelli singing love songs
Ever so distant they play in my head
I watch as you lay sleeping
Every breath you take I seem to take with you

This seems like yesterday, but I know better
So long ago, when everything was different
Love was so new and alive
I couldn't live without you
I didn't want to live without you
But so many things change, don't they
Time goes by as feelings do as well

But are they gone
I don't think they can dissipate that quickly
I still listen to Andrea Bocelli singing those love songs
I play them louder than life in my car
I want to remember those times with you
Keeping our Italian heritage, I can't let them end
It was real and alive and I think it will live on forever

Lying With You

Such a hard day today
Such a hard week last week
Do you wonder why I want to be in your arms?
When I am there, I am warm, cozy and comfortable.
I feel safe, warm, secure and loved
Nothing else matters to me
I love to lie there and watch you
As you doze off from working so hard, yourself
I see the soft smile sweetly planted upon your lips
I wonder what you're thinking as you are drifting off
I watch the shallowness of your breathing
The movement of your chest against mine
Oh, how I wish I were there at this moment
I need you in my life
I need you here with me
I need you to make my world a better place
My own safe haven
I long to go away with you
Time is of the essence
There is never enough of it to share
I just know where I want to be
Lying safely in your arms

Missing You Badly

I need you so badly right now.
I can close my eyes and taste your kisses
Kisses that no one before you ever could give me

Please take me in your arms and hold me
Hold me so close that I can feel your heartbeat
I want your heartbeat against mine.

To be wrapped up together as one
I need you more than you know
Please stop keeping yourself from me

My body longs for your sweet caresses
I need to hear your whispers
Just like those given to me once before

I try not to think of you constantly
Other men say words to me
Words I only want to hear from your lips
Not theirs

I long for that time that we will be together as one
Please don't make me wait forever
My heart will not follow another...not now
It is beating for you

Carol Livernois-Mitchell

Stolen Time

You can't go on stealing affections
Only when you have the time
It makes me feel bad, cause I don't have you
And wish, all the time, you were mine

The moments we share are all stolen
And never enough, I might add
Because of the distance between us
What we are doing, is bad

You need to do something about it
A decision by you must be made
For the hours that we've spent together
Were great, but to us were forbade

Please do put your life back together
Whatever decisions you'll make
I think you're a very nice person
Whatever you choose, I will take

Misty Kisses

For my special someone

Each drop of rain on my face
Is like a memory of you
The mist feels as new as morning dew
Those happy memories of sharing
So many raindrops
So much love
As I lift my face to the sky
I accept those gentle soft kisses of love
The anticipation of being with you
Once again, overwhelms me
To walk with you in that rain
Would be a dream
Holding hands
Caring
Sharing, misty kisses of love

My Angel

God sent me an angel from high up above
To help with getting over that awful last love
You were the one He picked significantly
To watch and share with and guard over me
You have me, you hold me and keep me so warm
You make me feel glad now, that I was once born
We have fun together whatever we do
I talk about most things, only to you
Thank you for understanding that my heart was so broken
You have my warmth and my friendship forever my token
Like flowers that grow to be what they are
We have each other's friendship that's growing by far
I'm glad that you want me, but please give me time
For once and for all I want someone to be mine
From today going forward I'm tired of being blue
Let's keep what we have here; I thank God for you

My Baby Girl Forever

What happened to that baby girl
She looked of porcelain with hair of night

What happened to my baby
That captured everyone's attention by her beauty

Where did my preschooler go with her ponytails
The one with flowing brown hair down her back

That baby girl with eyes as blue as a perfect sky
The princess that could steal your heart with her smile

My little one that spoke of only her truths
The ones that made everyone laugh because of honesty

That little baby I had that could make your heart melt
With words or a smile or maybe just a look

Where did my baby go that could tap dance
And make the prettiest ballerina not as pretty as she

Where is my baby that made my Mom's last days happy
The one that sat and entertained her Grandma every day

Where is that teenager that I had fun with, shopping
Going to lunch with, doing theater with

The teenager with only one boyfriend, who was everything
The one she stayed with for four years

I miss that little baby that I had
The one now that only seems to have problems

Problems that I am unable to fix anymore
The one that has hair of red from a jar

The child that doesn't seem to like me anymore
I miss my baby and I would really like to have her back

My very special baby girl

Carol Livernois-Mitchell

My Friend Michael

I met him on the Internet
Michael was his name
He used to email all the time
But now, he just plays games

I am jealous of where he lives
I'd live in Seabrook too
He says that he's romantic
But sometimes, makes me blue

I'd love the chance to meet him
Our heritage we share
He also likes to cook and bake
I wonder if he cares?

Time will tell just what I'll see
We'll give it just awhile
Now is time to close my screen
And put away this file

My Little Black Dress

Please come and put my hand in yours and let's go and dance
I've waited for so long for you to start this great romance
My little black dress is hung so neatly, tucked away in the closet
Just waiting for me to say I'm ready and that I have not lost it.

I haven't danced the night away in many, many years
I know that when I'm dancing, I have no time for tears.
Hold me close and we'll dance slowly, feeling our hearts beat as one.
The music will play and slowly we'll dance, not realizing when it is done

Do you feel the same as I do today, or am I in this all alone?
Please say that you are, cause I'd feel real bad if you gave me bad news on the phone
We'll dance until 2 or until we fall down, we'll laugh this whole night away.
We think the same thoughts, were brought up the same and I just can't wait for this day

So hurry and come here, I can't stand the wait
I've waited for you for so long
My little black dress and those high-heeled shoes are waiting to hear a good song!
My heart's crying out—No guys like to dance—what a shame in this life of mine?
I want you so bad, I love you so much and I'm not running out of good times!

Carol Livernois-Mitchell

Need, Want and Love

Happy birthday CDS, with much love

I want you
I want you so badly; I can taste you
I want to wake up with you at every new dawn
I want to touch you. I want to run my fingers ever so slowly over your face to feel who you are
I want to wipe the sweat from your brow
I want to read your eyes and kiss your sweet lips.
I want you
I need you
I need you so badly. I want to justify my love for you
A love that is so old, yet still burning in my heart
I need you to hold me so close that you will take my breath away
I need you to touch me, to hold my hand, to tell me how important I am to you
I need you to caress my body
I need you to read my thoughts
I love you
Three little words with such great capacity
I have loved you for years
The love that has been stored for so long needs to be set free
For no one knows me as well or ever will, as you do

Ninety Years Old

Dedicated to my Dad who passed away in 1976 and is missed very much

Today is your birthday, Dad
I wish you were here so I could make you a cake
I could put a corny little 'do-dad' on it
Oh how you loved the attention
Oh how I loved your excitement over the smallest details of living!
You would have been 90 years old today.
Ninety years old, Dad!
I'm willing to bet that you'd still be canoeing and trapping, hunting and fishing
You would still be so proud of your garden with the biggest tomatoes that
I have ever seen!
During your lifetime, you've reaped many benefits.
Being your daughter was great
I still miss you, after 24 years
I know the 'College of Hard Knocks' took more than four years to attend
You escorted me to a few of those courses
I'm glad that you did.
Although, physically you're not here today I'm singing *Happy Birthday* to you
In my heart
I only hope you can hear me

Nobody Knows, But You

When I talk with you, my heart races as fast as Nascars do
My heart flutters like twinkling stars
No matter what you look like, I love you!
How much one person can lift my spirits, no matter how 'down' I am feeling
How important it is that you always ask about my children
That my goal in my lifetime is to be a good mother
I can talk with you about *anything*
What I am thinking before I speak
That my heart has been put inside of "The Red Balloon" for safe keeping
How music is a significant part of my life
How much I once loved Patrick and Susan's father
How theater lets me avert my negative energies
How Ted broke my heart
How so many men have hurt me (On purpose? Who knows?)
That my job makes me want to quit working!
That holidays meant so much more when my parents shared them
How badly I feel that my baby brother doesn't talk to me
That my niece, Kathleen and nephew Ryan missed having a caring Aunt
That I have 'old fashioned' morals
That I'd rather give, than receive
How much I hate being FAT.
How I wish you lived closer to me
How I want to belong to you
Nobody knows, but you

Ocean Park

I wish you were here beside me
Sitting on this beach
I remember how I loved you
Cause you were just a peach

The statement of these ocean waves
Crashing in the sand
I close my eyes and think of you
And how our love was grand

The ocean meets the sky so blue
That's all the eye can see
I see you walking in the sand
Standing tall as you can be

I hope someday the time will come
When we can be alone
If you had not moved far away
You'd still call this your home

The more I write, the more I talk
The more I miss you so
If you come here anytime
I'll never let you go!

Carol Livernois-Mitchell

Once Upon a Heart

Once upon a heart
There was only You
Once upon a heart
I never felt so blue
Once upon a heart
I believed all that you said
Once upon a heart
I thought I'd used my head
Once upon a heart
You never told a lie
Once upon a heart
I never thought I'd cry
Once upon a heart
I was included in your life
Once upon a heart
Words never cut like a knife
Once upon a heart
My heart belonged to you
Now upon my heart
I don't believe it's true

One Fine Day

I saw you one fine day in Tennessee
Tall and handsome, like in my dreams
But you were real
I have known you for so long
Yet, I have just met you
Eyes as blue as the most perfect day
That perfect day in Tennessee
A perfect hug ensued
With kisses un-comparable to any
Soft spoken and so charming
The time was short
I will be back for missed time
I left a little piece of my heart with you
Guard it well, please keep it safe for me
As I am entrusting it to you
Perfect in my eyes, you are
I am coming back
To that perfect day in Tennessee
Yes, that one fine day

Open My Window

Your black and white plaid shirt
Hanging on my huge thick wood bedpost
Parked proudly under my window
When that window is open
The breeze carries through
That faint scent of you
Your cologne embedded into that shirt
That delicious smell of you
That shirt your wore so well
Now belongs to me
When I need you near me
I hold that shirt so close to my heart
I can almost feel your heartbeat
I can close my eyes and pretend
The arms of the shirt are wrapped around me
Like a whirling dervish, my thoughts are stolen
Just as you stole my heart so long ago
But you are gone now
I can only open my window
To have you near me

Please Whisper To Me

For you,Tim

Whisper is all I can do
Can you hear me; I think not
You were there and gone, now you've returned
Why is that? Are you drawn to me
For a particular reason
Is it the words spoken from my lips
Those words you long to hear
Those words I've not heard
Not since John left me
Please reach me, stretch as far as you can
Take me in your arms, hold me and let me know
Please whisper those words I long to hear
The whispers of lovers only for two
Brush your lips across mine
Whisper to me behind those doors
Secrets of only two; Only of us

Carol Livernois-Mitchell

Poems Prayers and Promises

Poems Prayers and promises
Are what life's all about?
I'm sure that you have been there
I have, without a doubt

Poems I write, prayers I've said
And promises I make
Are always there for them to use
Men use, abuse and take

My heart and soul are with that man
So very far away
I wonder if we'll ever meet
Or if I'm here to stay?

I just have this big old heart
That bleeds love all the time
But Mark will stay my special love
I wish that he were mine

He may be just like the rest
As far as I could know
Remember, he is married
But knows I love him so

Love and luck and sometimes lust
Is not at all for me
I might as well be by myself
I think that's meant to be

Pretty Soon

I sit here with my glass of wine
With fondest thoughts of you
You're life must be so very hard
With no home to go to

In just two weeks, all that will change
A place you'll call your own
You will be much happier
Life will have a different tone

Your friends will all support you
They'll stay through thick and thin
When they come knocking on your door
Be sure to let them in

My thoughts are always with you
Your friend, I am, it's true
I couldn't imagine what would be
If I did not have you!

Carol Livernois-Mitchell

Will I Make it?

Will I make it through this weekend?
My heart will be there with you
Your heart will be there with her
It just doesn't seem fair to me
I didn't want to feel this way
I really didn't want it to be like this
You will be unreachable to me
I have to ignore my feelings for two days
Will I make it?
Will I lie in bed at night wondering?
You know I will
Will I be wishing I were there?
You know I will
I promise I will try to ignore it all
That promise will be to myself
Alone, I will sleep
Will I make it?
Time will tell.

Quiet Sounds

Ah, that sound of quiet
The peace and tranquility of life
The leaves are gently swaying from a slight breeze
The breeze that brushes, ever so lightly across my face
But wait!
I now hear faded echoes of canine barks and yet in another territory
Two felines arguing
The sounds are ever so slight
If you listen, really listen
You hear far away, a faded montage of sounds
The beeping of a vehicle backing up, and engine revving, a car door closing
A distant chuckle and good-bye between friends
This wonderful sound of quiet
That I enjoy with a passion
I can even hear myself think
Isn't this a wonderful place to be?
Even if it is only, for a moment.

Carol Livernois-Mitchell

Remember I Care

Whenever you need me
I will be there
If you're feeling down
Remember, I care

I want to be with you
All of the time
Now and forever
I wish you were mine

I want you to hold me
Please, never let go
I'm lost in your kisses
And, loving you so

So in times of trouble
And when you feel blue
Remember I'm here
And my heart is with you

Reminiscing~

Written especially for CDS/Colorado Springs, CO

Please don't let the sun go down and take
away my shine
I remember years ago, when you were only
mine
And now I find you in my life, and happy
that you are
I feel like I should be outside, wishin'
upon a star
I close my eyes and feel you, holding me so
tight
Becoming one together, like eagles taking
flight
What did we know when we were kids, pushing
limits all the time?
I only know that in my heart, I was glad
that you were mine!

Scent of My Man

Another night alone
it is only one, of most
the scent of you remains here
it lingers upon my pillow
the creases in the sheets are pressed.
The scent fills the air
wherever I go, you are there
You are invisibly here
I will dream tonight, again
I will follow that scent
Physically, I will have you
I will dream that my hand is in yours.
You will embrace me
You won't leave me
The scent will remain...
Oh, that effervescent scent of you.

Secrets

Thank you for the night we shared
It meant so much to me
I really had a fun filled day
I knew that you could see

The tightness of your hold on me
Just really made my day
I felt the power ignite from you
In each and every way

This night was just so perfect
And secrets lit the night
We only had each other
We know it wasn't right

The gentle way you held my face
And kissed my lips so slow
My body was all-warm inside
And I could feel the glow

Flirting with the vision
Of you keeping me
Is something I must live without
I know it will not be

That night for us was special
We shared in every way
I hope you feel the same way too
We made each other's day

Carol Livernois-Mitchell

Shattered Dreams

Collective thoughts of you surround me like
a web of shattered dreams
The happy images that were once there, have
been eaten away
Consumed by some poison mass that one would
never have thought existed
Wanting to scream aloud, I find my words
buried beneath my vocal chords
The same vocal chords that once had nothing
but positive words
The web of deceit that you have built around
us needs to be destroyed, only by you
I need to escape your fortress before I can
no longer breathe
You have taken a piece of my heart
The piece that once was yours needs to be returned
Unless this love can be consummated, it has ended in that web of
Shattered dreams

Sidewalk Dance

I'm missing you real bad tonight, there's
fire in my heart
For if you weren't so far away, we wouldn't
be apart
The sidewalk dance was shared by us, no one
will ever know
The love I have within my heart, with
warmthness all aglow
No one saw us that warm night, except the
Man above
He has to know how hard it is controlling
this one love
I'll cherish that one moment, under that
bright moon
For that is my one promise, never popping
that balloon
I may be far away from you, but only miles
apart
For what I feel within my soul is measured
by my heart

Carol Livernois-Mitchell

So Many Stars

Thirty-five years ago we had our first date
We went to the circus. We sat so close in the back seat
Clutching hands, ever so tightly
Ever so young and so in love
You were my first love
So many stars and I chose you
What drew me to you? I don't know
So many things have happened over thirty-five years
Wives, husbands, children, loss of parents,
Loved in a different height
But it's not the same love
The love we shared
Young love
Not the love I hold in my heart and soul
Unconditional love we had for each other
How right your arms felt around me...No more
Those sweet kisses were always available...No more
Everything has changed now
I have my family and you have yours
We have memories that nobody shares but us
And I, being a woman am so good at pretending everything is okay

Some things are Better Left Unsaid

I saw your ad on the Internet
I answered you because you were a writer
I thought your brain was a step above the rest.
I thought we had something in common. Was I wrong!
We are not young anymore. We are not 16 or 20. Neither are we 30 or 40.
Our oats have already been sewn many years ago. Yet, we can still have a
great time and lots of fun.
I'm not saying we can't
You were my pleasure to meet, with your gorgeous smile. Your long hair meant
absolutely nothing to me. After all, I am a 60's child, ah, the good old days
neither was the fact that you were an Entrepreneur.
Why did you feel compelled to tell me that you have never dated 'heavy'
women before?
Thin ladies were your style. You told me also that this had changed recently.
You told me how wonderful your sexual experience was and how much you
enjoyed it.
Did it ever occur to you that some things are better left unsaid?
Why would I care how 'beautiful your special friend of American-Indian
heritage is and how you love taking her to dinner?
Why would I care about your 'afternoon delight' friend and the four hours she
spares you?
Some things are better left unsaid!
Yes, I enjoyed your company and I would like to see you again...as long as some
things are left unsaid!

Carol Livernois-Mitchell

Sunday Morning

On Sunday morning
I will wait for you
My body will be flirting with the thoughts of your embrace
I will be craving your affection
As the person craves his drug
I have missed you
I've missed my hand in yours
I have missed your sweet kiss and soft caresses
The strength of your manhood can hold a candle to none
I miss our conversations of importance and unimportance as well
I guess I just miss everything about you
I will wait for you
On Sunday morning

Thank You

We share many things
None of them are material
Your words are always adamant and encouraging
I wish I could comprehend everything the way you do
You always put situations in perspective
Something, I might add, that I couldn't do
You're always calm and understanding
How do you do that?
Please teach me
You are a good father
I'm on the outside looking in
I can only imagine what you were like when they were small
You are a kind person
Always there, if you can be, helping others to feel better
That's just how you are
What kind of Grandpa will you be?
A great one, I'm sure
You're a great friend
I'm just taking this time to let my feelings be known
Thank you for being my friend.

That Courtroom

I walked into that courtroom today for another time.
Oh how I dislike going in there
I think it is so demeaning to walk in there
I had no choice. My child was involved.
That child that I used to hold in my arms all the time
This was not going to be a good day. I just knew it.
The whole ordeal panned out very well for us in the end.
I am still upset to think that my baby that I always tried to bring up the correct
way was involved in something bad.
I supposed none of us is perfect.
There's no such thing as a perfect person, let alone a perfect child.
While sitting in that courtroom today
The officers brought out four children through a back door
Four children that could not have been more than 19 yrs old.
They were held behind a gate facing the crowded courtroom
My heart was aching
Imagine being one of their parents. How a parent must feel
I wondered if any of the parents were there at all
One was a girl and the rest were boys.
I wondered what she had done
What could have been so bad?
Shackles and handcuffs? Behind bars and locked doors?
Where could they go? They were locked in that corner
Society is so messed up. Courtrooms are a distasteful place to be
What is happening to our children?
I dislike the courtroom as I'm sure so many other do
I hope I never have to go there again and my heart is still aching for those four
children that I did not know.

That Rain

It sounds so very peaceful, not like my life
I hear the patter of that rain on the grass
outside my window...You are sound asleep
I hear the fullness of the deep breaths that
you are taking
You are hearing nothing and feeling at peace
Peaceful like the pattering of that rain
outside my window
I wish my being was feeling what you are at
this very moment
I feel revenge, torture, dislike, loneliness, depressed, untested
You haven't seen me for the past two months,
yet I remain here for you
I want to walk in the peacefulness of rain
I want that rain to come down on me as hard
as it can
I want to feel it hitting me in the face to
wake me from this nightmare
That rain...That peaceful pitter-pattering
of that rain

Carol Livernois-Mitchell

The Bought Oil Lamp

The oil lamp you bought last year
Is sitting here with me
The globe has been replaced two times
But at night at least I can see

The citronella smell emits
And chases away these bugs
I'm happy that you bought the lamp
If you were here, I'd give you a hug.

Although the oil is yellow
It's not a color I'd pick
Just yesterday I went to the store
To buy its second wick

So as you see, it's living on
Reminding me of you
If you hadn't left so abruptly
Then, we would still have you

The Poetess

With pen in hand memories put to paper

When you close your eyes you can pretend

You can pretend what you think the poetess looks like

Exactly how do you picture her to look?

Is she blonde, are her eyes big, is her hair long

Is she short, stout, tall, thin, pressed and creased to perfection?

Alas, you don't know her, only by her words

But you have created her in your mind

She is full of love, hope and passion

Wanting to share, she makes her pen keep no secrets

You know what she likes, she has told you, on paper

You know her thoughts, you've read what she's written

Yet, you do not know her, you just think you do

She is already created in your mind.

Will you be disappointed to find out that it is not how she looks

It is only her heart you know. Are you happy with that?

Are you eager to learn her more? Do you want her to pen about you?

Ask her. Find out what lies behind that paper and pen

you will be so very satisfied that you did.

The Real You

I wanted to run away with you to a place so far away
Just so we could be alone to have some fun and play
I got the hint just lately that you don't feel the same
Yet not too long ago, you wanted me to take your name

What have I done wrong to you that I don't know about
I was starting to feel comfortable, but now I have my doubts
Someone called the other night asking me to leave you alone
Thankfully the message was left because I was not at home

If I were here I would have said that you're her problem now
Of course for years I couldn't see that only love showed through some how
I would have told her how much you took and never wanted to give
And how long I put your family up with food and a place to live

With three of you and two dogs to boot, losing all my space
I thought it was very nice of me to offer to share my place
We're in this together, in the end it will all equal out
But retire with you are thoughts long lost and I definitely have doubts

You need to lose my number and never call my house
To me you've only used me and I think now you're a louse
Just pay me back the money that you so ignorantly borrowed
Now I know what you really are and for you I feel only sorrow

Think Twice

I left a message twice this week
But you did not call back
This relationship should be growing
But I think its sparks that lack

You have been most kind to me
A friend is always nice
We need to look more closely
I don't feel this will suffice

You always talk about Diane
And how you loved her so
It is time to now move on
You need to let her go

I know that love sometimes dies hard
And we don't want to let go
But if you think you care for me
It's time you let it show

Carol Livernois-Mitchell

Thirty-One Hours of Fantasy

Two consenting adults
No promises made, nor to keep
A secret shared by two
The burning desire
My hand fit into yours, like a glove
Our strides of walking were equal
Quiet thoughts read through eyes, only
Not many words spoken, but laughter was heard
Your body felt so right, there beside me.
Your skin felt perfect
The way you held my face, ever so gently
The perfect roughness of your hands touching my skin
How great that release felt
My heart, body and soul were taken by you at that compromising moment
It was right. There are no regrets.
Thank you for my fantasy~~~~
I will await the next

Too Young to Know About Love

If it wasn't love, what was it?
What was that feeling of fluttering inside my ever-so-young body?
But, I was only 15
I couldn't know what love was, so the adults told me
Infatuation they said; You'll get over it.
But when we parted, my heart fell
My soul was like a flower without rain
Drying up, wilting...dying
Wait!
There's that feeling again. I'm 16 now
Again the adults told me
You couldn't possible know what love is, you're too young
Today I am 50
I felt that 15 year old flutter again, just for a moment
"It can't be love," I said...
I'm too young to know what love is!

Carol Livernois-Mitchell

Watching You

I spent most of the night watching you sleep
I don't think you realize the stamina you have
Working so many hours during a week yet still having time for me
You looked so peaceful as I watched you
Your breathing mesmerized me
Your face looking so handsome as you slept
I could still see the child behind that handsome face
Sleeping so peacefully, I kissed your lips
You never moved, never flinched, just slept so peacefully
How I love to spend those moments watching you sleep
You looked so rested and comfortable
I cupped your face in my hands as I whispered softly to you
You never heard me speak
You never flinched, never made a sound
Oh, how I loved watching you sleep

Valentine's Day 2003

It's Valentine's day 2003
It's not with me you want to be
This is a very lonely day
For in the snow you want to play
Couples hold hands so lovingly
Are you happy you're not here with me
Does it make you feel good to ignore me now
To me this mess makes no sense, somehow
I guess up north is where you want to be
In your arms you should be holding me
That red woodstove will keep you warm
During the days thru the trails you will swarm
As you must know by now, I'm thinking of you
There's not been a moment I've not felt so blue

Carol Livernois-Mitchell

What Is

I looked into the mirror
And thought, what's this that I see?
I once looked so youthful
Is this really me?

I was once a beauty
Or at least my Dad said so
Now I don't like reflections that I see
With wrinkles that need to go

My hair once was real silky
Soft and dark and long
Doesn't have much gray in it
I guess I can't go wrong

My body needs some tending to
Chubby short and round
I guess I'll have to face it
That I am old age bound!

What Was

What was once
is not
The joy in your voice
is gone
The sparkle in your eyes
is dull
The happiness we once shared
is omitted
The kisses we shared
don't exist
The promise of tomorrow
has dissipated
The character you had
has diminished
The truths you told
Are now lies
What was once
is gone

Carol Livernois-Mitchell

Workaholic Larry

Larry, you're a special guy
Deep within my heart
Maybe someday we will meet
Although we're miles apart

Calls put in to me each day
Always make me feel good
And if I had to count on you
I know I surely could

Always busy with many jobs
With all those mouths to feed
You drive around for hours each day
For it's lots of money you'll need

The day will come when you can rest
But I think you need to teach first
Of all the time you've put into work
BK had to have been the worst

You have an education
And brains abound you so
I'm glad I found you that one night
To school you need to go!

I'll meet you on that balcony
The two of us will share
I'm glad to have you as my friend
You always show you care!

You Worry Me

You worry me
Thoughts of you fill my mind
Constant thoughts of you
I hear the unbalanced tone in your voice
Each time we talk your mood is inconsistent
I hear the ice in the bottom of that glass
What's in that glass won't make anything go away
Maybe it will be gone for a few hours
Tomorrow, things will be the same
I am here for you
I may not be an important part of your life, but I am here
I will listen to you
Please talk to me
You are too important to me
I don't' want anything to happen to you
The boys need you
Your parents need you
I need you. We love you
I worry always - - - -
You worry me

Carol Livernois-Mitchell

Messenger

You found me on the Internet
What did you think you'd see?
Of all the names and profiles
You ended up with me!

I do believe I'm flattered
There are so many names
I'm in here for good reasons
And it's not to play 'head games'

Although it took so long for us
In trying to connect
I saw you in my messenger
Try'n to interject

But now it comes this weekend
We've made a date to meet
It seems we've waited long enough
I really think it's neat!

Your Sweetie is Gone

I am so angry I can't even cry
The Lord knows how much I wish I could die
You took from me my heart and soul
And promised together, that we would grow old

See how you lie and turn things around
And most of the time you act like a clown
I try to forget you in my mind
The person you are is not very kind

Taking from everyone as much as you can
And I suppose you think that makes you a man
In my eyes for awhile you could do no wrong
Now I'm singing a whole different song

You live the same life you lived as a child
Not wanting to take a chance to go wild
I thought what we had could compare to none
And now I'm wishing that I had a gun

You were my love and my one and only
Now, all I feel is so sad and so lonely
So you have your friends, the few that you got
And kiss me good-bye, cause your Sweetie, I'm not

Carol Livernois-Mitchell

Your Love

+
Your love has captured my heart
Its hold so strong
Like a whirling dervish
Whisking me away
All too quickly
You have captured my very soul
And, I let it happen
I have dropped my shield
The armor has diminished
My will is free
Each breath I take whispers your name
I want you to love me as deep as the ocean
And I want you to want me
As bright as the sun
For your love has grasped my heart

About the Author

Born and raised in Marlborough, Massachusetts, I have always loved the Northeast part of the United States. I like the cooler weather therefore you are most likely to find me in New Hampshire or Maine. I did most of my writing for this book in Maine at either Pine Point, which is part of Scarborough, or at Ocean Park which is a quaint little area with it's own library and peaceful atmosphere. This book took me approximately five years to put together.

I graduated from the Marlborough Public School System in 1967 and took a business and computer class again in the beginning of 1990. I held many jobs, which always had to do with customer service, but always found myself writing whenever the spirit moved me. I might add that I was moved very often. Most of the time I was writing, came when I was in the beginning or end of a relationship. I had been married and I am the very proud mother of two children. I have a son that is a cook living and working in New Hampshire and a daughter that attends college at this time.

I grew up living in a Quonset hut that had an artesian well, taking a school bus to school every day. My parents worked in a shoe factory from 7 AM until 5 PM. When they returned from work, my duty was to have dinner on the table for them. I rarely missed a day. By the time I was 13, my parents had saved enough money to build a very small ranch house on our 21 acres, which had a cornfield in it. Every day the cows were brought to the pasture, across the street, by a neighbor that owned them, while I sat on the stone-wall, naming each cow. I grew up with lots of pets including bantam roosters, raccoons, rabbits, dogs, cats and guinea pigs. The street housed about nine houses, which were pretty far apart. We had two-party telephone lines. I did so much babysitting I already felt like a mother.

I had many hobbies from cooking, to shooting archery at our local Sportsman's Club to tap dancing and doing theater with disabled adults. I had a doll collection and even collected stamps when I bought milk in elementary school. Fishing was a big trip with my Dad. We both enjoyed salt-water fishing or deep sea fishing up north. I have one sibling, a brother that is younger than I am.

I wrote this book because I'm always looking to find my Prince Charming, only to find out down the road, that I am still left kissing the frog. Someday I hope that I will find that wonderful man riding in on the white horse to sweep me away. Until then, I can only put my feelings on paper, which is a talent that I have been blessed with. I have also been blessed with many friends who have encouraged me to publish my thoughts. I hope you enjoy them.